Please note the information contained within this document is for educational and entertainment purposes only. Every attempt has been made to provide accurate, up to date and reliable complete information. No warranties of any kind are expressed or implied. Readers acknowledge that the author is not engaging in the rendering of legal, financial, medical or professional advice.

By reading this document, the reader agrees that under no circumstances are we responsible for any losses, direct or indirect, which are incurred as a result of the use of information contained within this document, including, but not limited to, — errors, omissions, or inaccuracies.

Spanish

The Most Effective Way to Learn & Improve Your Spanish Language, Grammar, Writing Skills, & Vocabulary

Table of Contents

Introduction

Spanish is classed as one of the Romance languages. Of that group of languages, it's more widely spoke than any other, both in terms of the number of speakers and also the number of countries where it is spoken as a native language. Indeed, it's the most commonly spoken language around the world after Chinese and English. Spanish in South America is likely to be different to the Spanish spoken in Spain itself, and even there, there are different dialects. In this book, we'll be learning Castilian Spanish, which is the official language of the country, and that should enable you to be understood all over Spain, and probably anywhere else where Spanish is spoken. The differences aren't so significant.

The Romance languages all employ a fairly rigid word order within the sentences, and nouns are designated as either masculine and feminine, which determines the endings of accompanying adjectives, possessives and articles. Verb conjugation is one of the most important aspects of learning Spanish, but it is fairly straightforward, although there are a number of irregular verbs, which may take some time to get to grips with. Verbs are not gender specific, so one conjugation covers both sexes.

In many respects, Spanish is an easy language to learn, because the pronunciation is phonetic, and there are not so many vocabulary traps for the unwary, like there are in English. It has some peculiarities, like the fact that there are two verbs for 'to be,' 'ser' and 'estar,' each with different uses. And you don't need special vocabulary or verb tenses for questions, since the inflection of the voice identifies when you are asking a question as opposed to making a statement. All you need is the usual 'how, what, why, when and where?' and you're ready to ask a host of different questions in Spanish.

One significant difference between Spanish and English is the heavy use of the subjunctive mood, or using a verb to express doubt or uncertainty. It's also used to express feelings, and we'll look at it in more detail once you understand the basics of Spanish verbs. We don't want this to be more difficult than it has to be.

In Spanish, the adjective always precedes the noun, and the gender isn't always clear. For example, 'A blue dress' is 'Un vestido azul,' or 'A dress blue.' And just to confuse you, the Spanish word for dress – vestido - is in fact masculine! Just remember you don't ask for 'blanco/Rosado/tinto vino' – it's 'vino blanco/rosado/tinto.' It's important to get that one right, and in fact as you learn more Spanish it will come naturally to you.

If all this seems a bit confusing, you'll be pleased to know that you can usually manage with the present tense for verbs in conversational Spanish, so it's quite easy to get going with the language. In a week or so, you will probably mange to go into a shop or restaurant and order food and shopping, and maybe make small talk too.

This book will get you speaking and writing Spanish quickly, as well as helping you to improve your grammar and vocabulary. Whether you are new to the Spanish language, or aiming to become more proficient, you'll find all the help you need here, as well as a few things you probably never realized you needed. Buena suerte!

Chapter 1
Writing In Spanish

When you first start to build up your Spanish vocabulary, it's quite likely that you will understand more written Spanish than spoken dialogue. Native Spanish speakers are notorious for speaking very quickly – even when you ask them to slow down - and they tend to use their hands for punctuation as well as emphasis. It's a well-known joke that if you cut off a Spanish person's hands, they will not be able to speak! Yes, it's quirky and amusing, but it can also be very distracting, and more than a little intimidating, if you are trying to follow a conversation in Spanish.

You might want to start by reading in Spanish, to familiarize yourself with the vocabulary and sentence structure. The big advantage of reading written Spanish is that you can go over the words as often as you like, in your own time, until you are sure you understand it. In conversation, the words may be flowing at such a rate that you only catch one word in three or four. Reading in Spanish will build your confidence and increase your vocabulary before you actually try to have a real conversation with a native speaker – and his hands!

One thing that will strike you almost immediately is that Spanish punctuation and capitalization is nothing like what you have probably been used to as a native English speaker. For starters, there is the strange matter of the use of inverted question marks and exclamation points, which is unique to the Spanish language. To write down a question in Spanish, or to write an emphatic statement, it's customary to use an inverted question mark or exclamation point to start the sentence, then use a regular punctuation mark to close. So, 'Do you have a dog?' is written as:

¿Tienes un perro?'

And if you wanted to tell a friend in an email about your bargain from the local market, you would probably write:

¡Es tan barato! (It's so cheap!)

When you are speaking in Spanish, questions and emphatic statements are simply communicated by the inflection in your voice. There is no special vocabulary related to questions, other than the usual 'what, where, when, how, why?' suspects.

In written Spanish, accent marks called tildes are used to denote the correct pronunciation. If the accent is over a vowel, stress is placed on it to effectively lengthen the vowel. For example, in 'adiós,' (goodbye) the accent indicates that you should elongate and stress the letter 'o,' instead of making a short sound. Whenever you see a letter 'n' in a word with a little squiggle over it – as in 'mañana' (tomorrow, or morning) – the tilde serves to alter the pronunciation, and you would say 'manyana.'

In the Spanish alphabet, there are 27 letters – the usual suspects you know and love from the English alphabet, plus that ñ. In practice, the letters 'k' and 'w' are hardly ever used in Spanish words. In fact, 'w' is a late addition to the Spanish alphabet to accommodate foreign words. Spanish isn't big on the use of double consonants either – the only ones you will see are cc, ll, nn and rr. Those prolific ss combinations so beloved by English speakers never make an appearance in Spanish, and you may find that rather confusing until you get used to it – especially in written Spanish, because you'll have to suppress the urge to correct it.

Several common Spanish words consist of just a single letter – 'a' (to), 'y' (and) and 'o' (or) are the ones you will come across most often. It may seem a little strange at first if you are a native English speaker, where the only single letter English word is 'I.' In Spanish, it's 'yo,' and there's no capitalization, but very often, it's dispensed with, because the verb conjugation indicates the appropriate pronoun. There are lots of crafty little shortcuts in Spanish that will save you time and trouble, and you'll pick them up as you go along.

Another characteristic of the Spanish language is that the days of the week, months of the year, professions and nationalities are never capitalized. This only happens if such words occur at the start of a sentence, when the first letter of the first word of the sentence is capitalized, just as it is in English. You would therefore describe someone as 'español,' (Spanish) but if you were actually writing about their home nation, you would write 'España.' (Spain).

You need to be aware of these discrepancies when writing in Spanish, as you want to be sure to you convey the proper meaning. Spanish people, like most Europeans, are more relaxed about grammar and punctuation than their English counterparts, so don't be too concerned about it, but if you start off on the wrong foot, it's more difficult to 'unlearn' it later, so it makes sense to get it right from the start.

When you write a letter or an email in Spanish, you should use a colon, rather than a comma, following the salutation. Just as there are in English, there are formal and informal forms of salutation and closing to choose from, and you should select the appropriate form – it's good manners, and the Spanish are very big on that.

Informal salutations can be a simple 'Hola/ Hola a todos' (hello, hello everybody) or 'querido/a' (dear). You'd address Miguel as 'Querido Miguel,' and Silvia would be 'Querida Silvia.' The formal equivalent –also meaning 'dear' – is 'Estimado/a.' If you do not know who the letter is going to, it's 'A quien corresponda.' (To whom it may concern). Here are a few examples of appropriate Spanish salutations:

Hola Maria: - Hello Maria

Querido Juan: - Dear Juan

Estimada Sra Sanchez: - Dear Mrs Sanchez

If you wish to close a letter informally, use 'Cariños' (love) or 'Un saludo' (best wishes). If it needs to be more formal, use 'Atentamente,' (sincerely yours) or perhaps 'Saludos cordiales' (best regards). In the main text of the letter, you should refer to the addressee as 'tú' or 'usted,' depending on whether it's a friendly note or a business letter. Then check it through to make sure the salutation and the closing agree with the pronouns used in the body of the correspondence.

In general, there are not too many false friends in written Spanish. There are certainly far fewer homophones than there are in English. Homophones are words that sound the same, but have different definitions and may also be spelled differently, and there are a host of them in English, just waiting to trap the careless student or the unsuspecting traveller trying to impress his hosts.

Perhaps the most important homophone to get right is the distinction between 'el' and 'él,' particularly in written Spanish. 'El' means 'the,' but once accented, 'él' becomes 'he, him, or it.' When speaking in Spanish, the stress on the vowel is sufficient to differentiate between the two words, but when you're writing in Spanish, remember to include that all-important tilde, or you could change the entire context of the sentence.

One final thing to keep in mind when you are writing in Spanish is that the more extensive your vocabulary is, the more interesting and entertaining your written Spanish will be. Make it a habit to learn some new Spanish words every day. Why not make a list of 5 or 10 words, which you can learn and incorporate into sentences? It all helps to fix your brain into a Spanish mindset, which makes the learning so much easier – and much more fun. And if you're serious about learning Spanish, you need to be revising and learning new stuff on a regular basis, so think up activities to help expand your command of Spanish.

By now you should have picked up a few basic pointers on writing in Spanish, and you should be feeling more confident about using the vocabulary and grammar you have learned so far. Now let's take a look at some of the basics of conversational Spanish, so you can begin to speak, shop and socialize in your new language.

Chapter 2
Using The Verbs Ser And Estar

Before you can even begin to speak Spanish with any confidence, you need to get a grasp of how the verbs work, since they follow a strict conjugational form. However, before moving on to look at Spanish regular verbs, it's worth taking a look at how the verbs 'Ser' and 'Estar' are used, because you will be surprised how often they crop up in conversation. Also, if they are just lumped in with the rest of the verbs, you're going to find it confusing, so they deserve some special treatment.

The verbs 'Ser' and 'Estar' both mean 'To be,' but they are used in very different contexts. For native English speakers who are used to just one verb, this can seem a little strange, until you get used to when and how the two verbs are used. If you are eager to speak in Spanish as soon as possible, you need to get to grips with when and how to use these verbs.

'Ser' and 'Estar' are both irregular verbs, which means they do not follow regular verb patterns, so you really need to memorize them, since you are likely to be using them a lot in Spanish conversation. The good news is that, because they are in common use, they will soon be imprinted on your brain, and you will naturally select the correct verb and form. Here's the conjugation of both verbs, along with the English translation for comparison. Take as much time as you need to understand these conjugations. It's one of the most important and unique aspects of Spanish grammar.

To be	Ser	Estar
I am	Yo soy	Yo estoy
You are	tú eres	tú estás
He/she is	él/ ella/ usted es	él/ ella/ usted está
We are	Nosotros somos	Nosotros estamos
You (pl) are	Vosotros soís	Vosotros estaís
They are	Ellos/ellas/ustedes son	Ellos/ellas/ustedes están

In many cases, both verbs are used without the pronoun, which helps the flow of language, although sometimes the pronoun may be used for clarification. It's really down to personal preference and common usage. In the English language, the verb 'to be' is exclusively used in all contexts. However, in

Spanish, the verb selection depends very much on exactly what you want to say. When you're talking of a permanent state or a characteristic, you should use 'ser.' If someone wants to know your nationality, or if you want to tell anyone, you will say 'Soy ingles,' or 'Yo soy ingles' (I am English), because that will never change. (Note there is no capitalization in 'ingles.)

On the other hand, if someone enquires after your condition, what they really mean is how are you feeling at the time of asking, and that can and probably will change during the day. So, for example, you might say 'Estoy feliz,' or 'Yo estoy feliz.' (I am happy)

Note: I have used the verb with and without the pronoun here. Try both, and see which suits you best. Personally, I tend to dispense with it, and so do most of the Spanish people I know, but it's down to personal preference really. However, it does smooth the flow of conversation, and in fact little tricks like dispensing with pronouns and apocopation – which will be dealt with in more detail later – will help you to speak more quickly, which will increase your confidence.

Using Ser

As has been mentioned already, 'ser' expresses permanent states, or particular characteristics. That means you should use it to describe nationalities, and also characteristics of particular people or things. If, for example, a lady is particularly beautiful, you might say 'Ella es guapo,' since her beauty is a characteristic that is not going to change any time soon. She will still be beautiful next month, or next year, unless Fate intervenes in some way.

'Ser' is also customarily used for telling the time and mentioning the day or the date, talking about relationships and occupations, saying what something is made of, or where an event may be taking place, as well as denoting possession. Below are a few easy examples of the correct use of 'ser' in sentences. For ease of reference, and to make it easier to learn, the verb is always in italics.

La silla *es* de madera	The chair is [made] of wood
Qué hora *es*?	What time is it?
Soy el padre de Miguel	I am Miguel's father
Las	The pears are big

peras *son* grandes	
Soy medico	I am a doctor
Hoy *es* lunes	Today is Monday
El lapiz *es* de Maria	The pencil is Maria's
La fiesta *es* en el jardin	The party is in the garden

You may have noticed that the most frequently used forms of this verb happen to be 'soy' and 'es.' Since they are widely used in Spanish conversation, it's important to know how to use this verb correctly. When you have learned 'ser,' you will be able to discuss the time and date, your occupation, and your personal and family relationships. You will also be able to talk about the composition and ownership of a number of items, so just learning how to use 'ser,' along with some simple vocabulary, will open up a number of avenues of conversation.

If you're somewhat confused by this, and you're thinking that occupations and relationships may not be permanent – you can change your job at some point, and you could fall out with your significant other – well, up to a point, that's true. However, to make it easier, think of your job and your relationship as part of you, and you, in essence, are 'soy.'

Using Estar

As has already been noted, 'estar' denotes the temporary condition of something or someone, as opposed to a permanent state. Put simply, if you are enquiring after the welfare or condition of a person or thing, you will use 'estar,' and the other person will use it in their response to your enquiry. 'Estar' is also customarily used to denote physical and geographical locations, although not your home nation, or where an event is taking place. So you might say 'Soy de Italia,' (I am from Italy), but 'Italia está en Europa.' (Italy is in Europe.)

'Estar' is also used in idioms – For example, 'Estar de camino' is 'To be on the way.' The verb is not as widely used as 'ser,' however it is imperative that you know exactly when and how to use both verbs. Below are some simple examples of the uses of 'Estar' in context. Again, the verb is in italics for ease of reference.

Spanish	English
¿Cómo *estás* usted?	How are you?
Estoy muy bien, gracias	I am very well, thank you
¿Donde *está* la peluqueria?	Where is the hairdresser's salon?
El estofado *está* muy caliente	The stew is very hot
Estoy de camino	I am on the way

These are the most common usages of the verbs 'Ser' and 'Estar,' with simple contextual examples. Try to construct simple sentences where you will be able to use one or the other in conversation, and make up some questions and answers to use other parts of the verbs. This will help to increase your vocabulary, as well as teaching you how to differentiate between the two very different versions of 'To be.'

Chapter 3
The Different Types of Spanish Verbs

Verbs – or 'doing words,' as our Elementary School teachers were wont to describe them - form the cornerstone of all languages, and Spanish is no different. If you want to converse and write in Spanish, one of the first things you need to do is to discover how the different verbs work. All Spanish verbs are extensively conjugated, and that may seem a bit scary when you first begin to learn the language. However, there are rigid rules which cover conjugation, and the verbs tend to sit mainly in broad categories depending on their endings and the way they are conjugated, so once you learn how it all works, you can pretty much conjugate any verb.

All Spanish verbs slot into three main categories, with their own specific features and rules. The main types are regular verbs with different endings, irregular verbs, and the rather quirky stem-changing verbs. Let's look at them in the order in which you need to learn them.

Regular verbs

Regular verbs follow a regular pattern of conjugation, which is always determined by the last two letters of the verb in its infinitive form. There are three endings for all Spanish verbs, whether they are regular, irregular or stem-changing, and those are −ar, -er, and −ir. To conjugate any verb, just remove the two letter ending, then add the appropriate pronoun and suffix. The pronouns necessary for verb conjugation, which are also used for addressing and referring to different people, are as follows:

Spanish	English
yo	I
tú	You (singular, informal)
usted	You (singular, formal)
él	he
ella	she
Nosotros/nosotras	We (masculine/ feminine)
Vosotros/vosotras	You (plural, informal,

	masc./fem.)
ustedes	You (plural, formal)
Ellos/ellas	They (masc./fem.)

It's worth pointing out here that in normal Spanish conversation, the pronoun is usually dispensed with, unless it is needed for clarity or to emphasize a point. You can just use the conjugation of the verb. For example, 'I have two sons' can be 'Yo tengo dos hijos' or 'Tengo dos hijos.' Either form is grammatically correct, but version two is more likely to come from the mouths of native Spanish speakers, so that's the one to go for.

Also, notice that the formal pronouns 'usted' and 'ustedes' are not conjugated in the same way as 'tú' and 'vosotros.' This preserves the distinction between formal and informal address, and makes it immediately obvious to whoever you are speaking to. It's important, because although the Spanish people are very laid back in many ways, they are pretty hot on getting the formalities right, and will notice if you get it wrong.

To conjugate Spanish verbs, remove the final –ar, -er or –ir - then attach a new suffix to the stem of the verb. This suffix will be determined by the final two letters of the verb in its infinitive form, and which category the verb falls into.

Spanish verbs have several different tenses, very much like English verbs. However, if you can familiarize yourself with the present tense, you will be able to converse quite well. That's because the present tense of Spanish verbs actually has three different meanings. If we use the verb 'comer' (to eat) as an example, you can see how it works 'Yo como,' or 'Como,' means 'I eat.' It also means 'I am eating' as well as 'I do eat.' Therefore you have a lot of potential conversation at your disposal if you are able to confidently conjugate Spanish verbs in their present tense.

When you have learned to conjugate a single regular verb from each of the three infinitive forms, you will be able to conjugate all regular verbs using that as a pattern. You just need to learn the verb endings, and they will imprint themselves on your mind with regular use. As an illustration, let's look at three of the most commonly used Spanish verbs: comer (to eat), hablar (to speak), and vivir (to live). Since everyone, everywhere, has to eat, speak and live, you'll be able to make a number of conversations from that!

Below are those three conjugated verbs, presented in table form along with their accompanying pronouns, to make it easy for you to refer back to them when you need to. However, you'll be surprised how quickly you'll get the hang of conjugation once you've had plenty of practice.

Pronoun	Hablar	Comer	Vivir
Yo	hablo	como	vivo
tú	hablas	comes	vives
Él/ella/usted	habla	come	vive
Nosotros/as	hablamos	comemos	vivimos
vosotros	habláis	coméis	vivís
Ellos/ellas/ustedes	hablan	comen	viven

It makes sense to learn the verb conjugations in the same order that they are listed above, since the majority of regular verbs end in –ar. Considerably fewer end in –er, and the smallest group of regular verbs are the ones ending in –ir. As soon as you are confident with conjugating an –ar verb automatically, you can move on to the –er verbs, and finish up with the –ir group. Don't try to rush the verbs – the more time you spend on them, the more easily and quickly you will be able to converse in Spanish.

Consider investing in a quality Spanish verb reference book. Not only will it provide you with a comprehensive list of verbs to augment your vocabulary, it will also give conjugations of other tenses, as well as supplying hints and tips on using Spanish verbs both in conversation and in writing. I find that the Collins series of bilingual dictionaries are excellent for this purpose, but there are lots more available. The Santana book *Simplified Spanish Verbs* is another excellent book that is recommended by many Spanish teachers. Check out a few Amazon reviews as a starting point. I would recommend that you purchase at least one verb reference book that you can dip into periodically for practice, or to find the right verb for your needs in any situation, whether you are conversing or writing.

Irregular verbs

With most things in life, there are exceptions to the most rigid of rules, and this also applies to Spanish verbs. Irregular verbs might have different endings in each of the conjugations, or they may only vary in the first person (yo) conjugation. The main problem here is, you can't tell simply by looking at a Spanish verb whether it is regular or irregular. That means you will need to familiarize yourself with all the irregular verbs, and also the appropriate conjugations. You should probably leave this until you're completely happy with conjugating regular verbs. Annoyingly though, some of the more frequently used verbs also happen to be irregular. Commonly used irregular verbs include ir (to go), plus ser and estar, which have already been discussed in depth.

Ir is a verb that is frequently used in conversation. In addition to the obvious going places, where you would use ir – including the beach, school, a restaurant, the theatre, a destination – when you say you're going to do something, you will also use ir plus an infinitive. 'I'm going to drive to the town' would be 'Voy conducir a la ciudad.' This is an excellent illustration of one of the alternative meanings of the Spanish present tense, 'I am going.' Here's how you conjugate ir:

Yo voy	I go/am going/ do go
Tú vas	You go, etc
Él/ella/usted va	He/she/you formal go, etc.
Vosotros vais	You (pl informal) go, etc.
Nosotros vamos	We go, etc.
Ellos/ellas/ustedes van	They/you (pl. formal) go, etc

A common use of ir is in first person plural, where 'Vamos' means 'let's go,' and dispenses with the pronoun. So 'Vamos al cine' could be 'We are going to the cinema' or 'Let's go to the cinema,' depending on how you say it. The Spanish language is like the people - very free and easy. That makes it much easier to pick up than many languages, which means you can get started on basic conversation fairly quickly.

To a degree, irregular verbs do tend to follow a pattern of sorts, since verbs with the same endings will often be conjugated in the same manner. Without getting bogged down in the theory of irregular verbs, here are a few pointers to help you spot irregular verbs. Check out the various conjugations in your verb book – it's certain to contain a section devoted to irregular verbs. Alternatively, you can search for conjugations online.

A number of important irregular verbs only conjugate irregularly in first person singular form (yo). The remainder of the conjugation follows the same pattern as regular verbs. For example, the verb 'dar' (to give) starts as 'Yo doy' in first person, and then reverts to the regular –ar conjugation model of 'hablar.' It's useful to know that 'Poner' (to put) and 'hacer' (to make, or to do) conjugate as 'Yo pongo' and 'Yo hago' respectively in first person singular, after which they follow the regular –er conjugation pattern exemplified in 'comer.'

Hacer is handy to know, since it's the verb of choice when taking photographs, which everyone does, all the time 'Hacer photo' means to take a photograph, although 'Hago photo' is literally 'I make, or I am making a photograph.' However, it's how the natives say it, so it's how you should say it.

Other frequently used verbs which are only actually irregularly conjugated in the 'yo' form are 'ver' (to see) and 'saber' (to know). Here, the respective first person conjugations are 'Yo veo' and 'Yo sé.' You might find it helpful to make a list of this type of irregular verb, and check it regularly until the details are fixed in your head.

Another pointer towards irregular verbs is in the final letters of the infinitive form, before the –ar, -er or -ir. When a verb infinitive form ends with a vowel, followed by the letters –cer, - cir or –ducir, it's irregular, but only in the first person conjugation. The final letters will be replaced by –zco for first person singular, and the other parts of the conjugation will follow the pattern of regular –er and –ir verbs. To illustrate how it works, here's the conjugation for two commonly used irregular verbs - 'conocer' (which means to know, particularly when referring to a person), and 'conducir' (to drive). This pattern can be followed to conjugate any and all verbs which end in a vowel followed by -cer or -cir.

Conocer	Conducir
Yo conozco	Yo conduzco
Tú conoces	Tú conduces
Él/ella/usted conoce	Él/ella/usted conduce
Nosotros conocemos	Nosotros conucemos
Vosotros conocéis	Vosotros coducís
El/ella/ustedes conocen	El/ella/ustedes conducen

Please don't worry too much about how irregular Spanish verbs work. Learn them, or better yet, learn how to recognize them. Most of them are not quite as irregular as you may initially believe!

Stem-changing verbs

Spanish irregular verbs are those verbs where the ending changes on conjugation. Generally, this only applies to first person singular (yo). In stem-changing verbs, it is the stem – or the part of the verb that comes before the –ar, -er or –ir – that actually changes, with the exception of the notostros/vosotros form, when the stem is unchanged. The verb endings adhere to the regular verb conjugation model.

You will never be able to recognize a stem-changing verb by its appearance, therefore you will need to learn them, and also learn how they are conjugated. There are three main forms of stem change you need to be aware of. Generally, stem changes concentrate on a stressed letter 'e' or 'o' in the stem. If there happen to be two of them in the stem, it's the second letter that's earmarked for change. The 'e' changes to either 'ie' or 'i,' and the 'o' will change to 'ue.' One exception to this rule is the verb 'jugar.' (to play) In this case, the 'u' changes to 'ue' in the stem. This is the only verb that behaves in this way, so it's well worth remembering.

Here are a few examples of conjugation models for stem-changing verbs. They are some of the more frequently used verbs. 'Querer' (to want, or to love) is an e > ie stem change, while 'dormir' (to sleep) undergoes an o > ue change, and 'servir' (to serve) is an e > i stem change.

Querer	Dormer	Servir
You quiero	Yo duermo	Yo sirvo
Tú quieres	Tú duermes	Tú sirves
Él/ella/usted	Él/ella/usted	Él/ella/usted

quiere	duerme	sirve
Nosotros queremos	Nosotros dormimos	Nosotros servimos
Vosotros queréis	Vosotros dormís	Vosotros servís
Ellos/ellas/uste des quieren	Ellos/ellas/uste des duermen	Ellos/ellas/uste des sirven

It should be noted at this juncture that 'querer' is a verb you will use a lot, whether as an expression of affection or when ordering dishes from a menu, or making purchases in the market or in a store. If you want to say 'I love you very much,' it's 'Te quiero mucho,' while 'Quiero un kilo de patatas' is 'I'd like a kilo of potatoes.' Querer is a very useful verb to have under your belt, because it's the simplest way to request items in a bar, restaurant or shop, and it's also the language of love!

Tener and venir

Before moving on from the topic of stem-changing verbs, two verbs deserve a special mention in despatches. 'Tener' (which means to have) and 'venir' (to come) are used frequently in Spanish, and not always in ways you might expect. Tener is typically used to denote age, feelings and ownership. You might say 'Tengo una casa en el pueblo (I have a house in the village), 'Tengo cuarenta años' (I am 40 years old), or 'Tengo sed' (I am thirsty). In the second and third examples, you are literally saying 'I have 40 years' and 'I have thirst.' It may seem strange at first to English speakers who are used to saying 'I am' in these circumstances, but it's the way it's done in Spanish, and you'll soon get the hang of it.

Venir is customarily used to reflect time in the future. The Spanish word 'proxima' means 'next,' so if you wanted the next station on the railway line, you would ask for 'Proxima parada.' On the other hand, if you need to make an appointment for the following week, it's customary to say 'La semana que viene' - literally 'The week that comes.' You will certainly be understood if you say 'Proxima semana,' but it's preferable to learn to speak like the natives do right from the start. Here are the conjugation models for 'tener'and 'venir.'

Tener	Venir
Yo tengo	Yo vengo
Tú tienes	Tú vienes
Él/ella/usted tiene	Él/ella/usted viene
Nosotros venemos	Nosotros tenemos
Vosotros tenéis	Vosotros venís

| Ellos/ellas/ustedes tienen | Ellos/ellas/ustedes vienen |

A word about verb moods in Spanish

When people speak of the 'mood' of a verb in any language, they are not talking about whether they are having a bad day or a good day and the resulting feelings they are experiencing. The mood of the verb indicates the way it is being used and perceived. A mood has nothing to do with the tense of the verb – that is in the past, the present or the future, and it refers to something that has, is now, or will be taking place. It's the action of the verb, whenever occurs. The mood refers to the perception or purpose of the verb's action.

There are three moods that are commonly used with verbs in Spanish – the indicative, the subjunctive and the imperative. Briefly, the indicative is the mood to use with facts, the subjunctive is used whenever there is an element of doubt or subjectivity, and the imperative is used for commands. A good grasp of the use of moods will help you to communicate more effectively.

Indicative and Imperative moods versus subjunctive mood

The indicative and imperative verb moods are fairly simple to sort out. Indicative is about statements, facts and certainties. If you say 'Leo el libro,' you are telling whoever is interested that you are reading the book. That's a fact which can be verified, and it's a statement of your actions. It's also the verb in its indicative mood. If however, your teacher is ordering you to read a book you are trying to avoid reading, she would say '¡Lee el libro! (Read the book!). That's the imperative mood in action. On the other hand, it may not be possible to read the book right now, so you may say 'Leyere el libro.' (I will read the book).

That's the subjunctive at work, because although you intend to read the book at some point in the future, it's a wish or a hope, rather than a fact. Things could change, and while the indicative of the verb states the fact that you are reading the book, and the imperative is an exhortation to read the book, the subjunctive is an expressed hope to read it – it's not a concrete fact, it's an abstract wish.

As has already been briefly mentioned, the subjunctive mood is used to indicate doubts, feelings and even wishes for things to be different to the way they are. This applies whether the action of the verb is in the past, the present or the future.

The subjunctive mood is infrequently used in English, but it's very common in Spanish, so although you can converse without using it at all, it will open up so much more of the language if you can get a grip on the subjunctive as well.

Spend plenty of study time on learning Spanish verbs and their conjugation models, because it is a major component of learning the language. If you can get the verbs right, everything else will fall into place around them. And when you are feeling more confident with the verbs, take a look at the moods – particularly the subjunctive mood – and see if you can learn to use it in conversation. Don't be afraid of Spanish verbs – embrace them, and make friends with them. They are your passport to speaking Spanish!

Chapter 4
Ways To Expand Your Spanish Vocabulary

By now, you should have a good grasp of Spanish verbs, whether regular, irregular or stem-changing. If you've got on really well, you may even have dabbled a little in the subjunctive verb mood. However, man (or woman) cannot converse with verbs alone, so now it's time to expand your vocabulary. You need to learn new nouns, adjectives, adverbs and prepositions, in order to be able to converse and write in Spanish without sounding stilted or boring.

A good way to increase your vocabulary fairly quickly is to work with themes. For instance, one day, you could learn most of the words you would need to order food and drinks in a restaurant, and make small talk with your waiter. Tomorrow, you may decide to learn useful words for when you want to say 'Vamos a la playa' (Let's go to the beach). If you're planning a trip to the Mercado (market), you might want to concentrate on learning the names of various fruits and vegetables, and items of clothing and household goods.

Colors and numbers also need to be learned, since they crop up with surprising regularity in conversation. Go back to your childhood days and count your steps as you walk, or your strokes as you swim, in order to practice your Spanish numbers. They are not difficult to learn, and if you use them regularly, they will soon be enshrined in your memory. Try and think of more creative ways to practice your Spanish numbers, such as playing bingo with family and friends. If it's fun and interesting to learn, it sticks in your mind much better than if you try to learn by rote.

It's useful to know the Spanish words for various items of clothing, and if you pair them up with different colors, you will find it easier to remember the words for both clothes and colors. Don't forget that in Spanish, the adjective always follows the noun. Also, the color takes on the gender of the noun, so you might try on 'Una falda roja' (A red skirt) or 'Un vestido Amarillo (A yellow dress). If you get it wrong, you will still be understood, but as we have said before, it's easier to get it right from the start than it is to 'unlearn' a mistake.

An excellent way to learn vocabulary and absorb Spanish culture is to take a wander around the local street market. The items on sale will all be labelled, allowing you to visually associate the

Spanish word with the item – rather like flash cards for grown ups. Be sure to buy a few things and practice your Spanish – it's the only way to learn the language and improve on your skills.

When you're shopping, remember that the verb 'Querer' means to want, as well as to love, therefore 'Quiero un kilo de manzanas' is 'I want a kilo of apples.' It doesn't mean you have professed your undying love for a Golden Delicious! Don't be afraid to try out your Spanish, even if you sometimes get it wrong. It will be noted and appreciated that at least you tried, and you will receive excellent service as a result. And if you make mistakes and are corrected, it will stay in your brain, particularly if the mistake caused a measure of amusement! No matter how long you spend with books and language CDs, the only effective way to gain confidence and fluency in the language is to use your Spanish vocabulary on a regular basis, and in a variety of situations, so you get plenty of practice.

Another way to expand your Spanish vocabulary is to pick up special offer leaflets from various stores. Almost always, the pictures are accompanied by words, and that helps you to fix them in your mind. It's yet another version of flash cards for grown ups – associating words with pictures. It works for children, and it will work for you too. Most of the major supermarkets issue new flyers each week with their special offers listed, so be sure to check them out on a regular basis.

Another fun way to increase your vocabulary is to write down words on small cards along with their English translations, then try to make sentences using your words by shuffling the cards around. Phrase books have their uses, but they'll never help you to speak and write in Spanish. They are intended to help you get by if you don't speak the language, or to help out in an emergency situation, not for the mundane, everyday stuff of conversations. If you are serious about learning Spanish, and want to improve as you go, you need to be constructing your own sentences using the words that are relevant to your particular situation. That's the only way to really learn and understand how the language works.

Another interesting and fun way to boost and improve your Spanish vocabulary is to contact native Spanish speakers online who wish to improve their English. Message each other, each using the other's native language. So, you would ask a question in Spanish, and your online friend would reply in English. Each of you can offer advice and encouragement on your friend's grasp of the language.

As has been noted previously, it's much easier to cope with simple written sentences in the early stages of learning in Spanish, and bilingual chatting online will give you the confidence to progress with your conversational Spanish. You have time to check over the messages, and maybe look up the words you haven't come across before. Keep a notebook and pen beside you as you chat and jot down new words and ideas that spring from the conversation – you'll be surprised how much new knowledge you can pick up from a single online chat.

You can take this to the next level, by taking part in an intercambio. That's a live version of the online chat, where you meet up with other people and converse in each other's language. It's great fun, and long lasting friendships can be forged as you expand your Spanish vocabulary and polish up your grammar.

The secret to expanding your Spanish vocabulary isn't really a secret at all – it's common sense. As you learn new words and phrases, write them down so you can familiarize yourself with them. The visual confirmation of how you are progressing will also encourage and motivate you to learn even more. You also need to find as many opportunities as you can to speak and read Spanish. Make that your mission, and you will soon become more fluent and more confident when speaking in this beautiful language.

Chapter 5
Prepositions and Directions

Once you have a firm grasp of the basics of verbs, adjectives, numbers and colors in Spanish, you can think about adding more to your store of knowledge with a few prepositions – in, on, under, on top of, and other 'positional' words – and directions. It's surprising how often you find yourself either asking for or giving directions – unless you're a man, of course, in which case you never, ever ask for directions! For everyone else though, directions are useful to know and, along with prepositions, they can significantly increase your potential for both speaking and writing in Spanish.

One major difference between English and Spanish prepositions is that one Spanish word can cover a number of different meanings and contexts. The only way to get a grip on this is to use the prepositions in the way the Spanish use them. It's a question of research and practice. Don't be intimidated, because you'll soon get the hang of using prepositions the way the Spanish use them.

Some prepositions need more explanation than others, because they have a wider variety of uses. Two of them – 'de' and 'a' – merit closer attention before moving on to the rest.

Using the preposition 'de'

Prepositions can be tricky in Spanish until you get used to them, because often, they have more than one meaning. An obvious example is 'de,' which can mean of, made of, from, or about. It's also customarily used to denote possession and origins, and it's used in superlatives. Perhaps the easiest way to demonstrate how 'de' is used is to offer some examples.

Spanish	English
El coche rojo es de Maria	*The red car is Maria's (of Maria)*
La buffanda es de algodon	*The scarf is cotton (made of cotton)*
Soy de Italia	*I am from Italy*
Ella es la mas hermosa de todas	*She is the most beautiful of them all*
Leo un libro de cocina	*I am reading a cookery book (book*

52

	about cookery
Bebo un vaso de sangria	*I am drinking a glass of sangria*

For ease of understanding, the literal translations are included in brackets, after the broad meanings of the sentences. Practice using 'de' in written sentences to familiarize yourself with this important and versatile Spanish preposition.

Using the preposition 'a'

Another versatile and widely used preposition is 'a.' It's English equivalent is to or at, but like 'de,' it can be used in various ways, not all of which are immediately obvious. However, as you become more proficient at Spanish, you will soon learn how and when to use 'a' in its customary contexts.

The main uses of 'a' are to denote time, movement, location, the way things are done and price, so it can mean towards and for, depending on the context. It can also be used to mean on, by, from, with, into, or in, among other things. Again, it's simpler and quicker to show how 'a' is used, so here are some examples, with English translations.

Spanish	English
Vengo a las once	*I'll come at 11 o'clock*
Vamos al mercado	*We're going to the market*
La puerta a la cocina esta abierta	*The door to the kitchen is open (you could also use 'de' here)*
Voy a bailar con mi marido	*I am going to dance with my husband*
Lavamos el coche a mano	*We'll wash the car by hand*

In the sentence 'Vamos al Mercado,' al is used as a contraction of 'a el,' which would be awkward to say. You should always use 'al' with masculine objects. So you would say 'Vamos al cine,' or 'Let's go to the cinema,' but 'Vamos a la playa.' (Let's go to the beach). La playa is feminine, so there is no contraction.

There is another special use of 'a,' which you will notice in the above examples. It's also used together with the verb 'ir' and the infinitive when you want to express a future intention. Although the infinitive form bailar means 'to dance,' it's customary to use 'a' as a bridge between the verbs. Literally, the sentence reads 'I am going to to dance with my husband.' It's one of a number of quirks of the Spanish language that doesn't have an English equivalent.

The Personal A

Speaking of things with no English equivalent, no discussion on Spanish prepositions is complete without reference to the use of the Personal A. In English, there is no difference in the sentence structure whether the verb refers to a person or a thing, but in Spanish, anything referring to a specific person or domestic pet – whom many people think of as persons in their own right – is preceded by the Personal A.

Confused? There's really no need to be! Let's assume you number a hairdresser among your friends and acquaintances. It's accurate to say:

Conozco a una peluquera – *I know a hairdresser*

However, if you're in need of a quick wash and blow dry, but don't have a particular hairdresser in mind for the job – maybe your hairdresser friend isn't very good – then you would say:

Necesito una peluquera – *I need a hairdresser*

Your hairdresser acquaintance is a specific person, so she gets a Personal A, but the required hairdresser could be anybody, so there's no need to use it.

When it comes to animals, use the Personal A for dogs and cats and other domestic pets, but not for animals in general. So, assuming you are walking your dog in the fields, and you spot some cows, this is how you'd describe it:

Puedo ver a mi perro, Pedro –*I can see my dog, Pedro*

Puedo ver tres vacas – *I can see three cows*

Pedro gets a Personal A because he's part of the family, but the cows are not domestic animals, so they don't warrant it.

It's a good idea to spend some time working with the Personal A, so that its uses are clear in your mind. Getting it right shows that you are serious about learning Spanish, and like many Spanish grammar rules, it's fairly straightforward once you get used to it. And you will certainly impress your Spanish friends if you can drop in a Personal A when it's appropriate.

Other prepositions

Most other Spanish prepositions are similar to their English counterparts in that they are used in specific instances. Here's a list of them, with examples of how to use them.

Spanish	English	Example of use
Antes de	Before	Antes de comemos, lavamos nuestras manos

		Before we eat, we wash our hands
Bajo	Under	El gato está bajo la silla *The cat is under the chair*
Cerca de	Near	El coche está cerca de la casa *The car is near the house*
Con	With	Prefiero tortilla de española con cebollas *I prefer Spanish omelette with onions*
Delante de	In front of	El perro está delante de la casa *The dog is in front of the house*
Dentro de	Inside	Mi padre es dentro de la iglesia

		My father is inside the church
Desde	Since, from	Desde el lunes, sera muy calor *From Monday, it will be very hot*
Despues de	After	Después de comer, quieremos hablar *After eating, we like to talk*
Detras de	Behind	El perro está detrás de la silla *The dog is behind the chair*
Durante	During	Durante agosto, hace muy calor *During August, it is very hot*
En	In, on	El vino está en la nevera

		The wine is in the fridge
Encima de	On top of	El plato está encima de la mesa *The plate is on top of the table*
Enfrente de	In front of	Mi coche está enfrente de mi casa *My car is in front of my house*
Entre	Between	Entre las dos y las tres, caminamos el perro *Between two and three, we walk the dog*
Fuera de	Outside of	El gato está fuera de la tienda *The cat is outside of the store*
Hacia	Towards	Conduzco hacia la cuidad

		I am driving towards the town
Hasta	Until	Hasta luego, mi amigo *Until later, my friend*
Para	For, in order to	El regalo es para mi *The gift is for me*
Por	For, by	Muchas gracias por la cena *Thank you very much for dinner*
Según	According to	Según mi hermano, el bar está cerrado *According to my brother, the bar is closed*
Sin	Without	Voy sin mi hija *I am going without my daughter*

Sobre	Over, about	Es una pelicula sobre la guerra
		It's a film about the war

Just a point of interest to note here. You may have noticed the use of 'es' rather than 'está' in the sentences 'El regalo es para mi' and 'Es una pelicula sobre la Guerra.' That's because these are permanent states – the gift will always be mine, and the film will always be about the war. However, the cat will not always be outside the store, and the wine will not always be in the fridge.

When to use 'para' and 'por'

Before we move on from prepositions to directions, something else warrants more explanation. You will see that there are two words for 'for' – 'para' and 'por.' They each have their particular uses, and if you're serious about learning Spanish, you need to know the difference.

'Por' can also mean by, along, through, and about, so it is used to describe transport and movement methods, among other things. For example, if you wanted to say 'I am going to Barcelona by train,' you would say, 'Voy a Barcelona por tren.' If you're on the market, you may see a sign on the lechugas (lettuces) 'Cuatro por €1' (4 for €1).

'Para' is more commonly used for lots of scenarios. If something is intended for a particular person, it will be para, rather than por. When you order in a restaurant, you will say, 'Paella para mi' (Paella for me) – or whatever you're having. And in the example above, 'El regalo es para mi.' (The gift is for me). If there is a specific person or purpose, it's para, but if it's not so clear, it's por.

Now you have a list of Spanish prepositions, along with examples of how to use them, and explanations of common uses. Prepositions are very important in several aspects of Spanish conversation, and one area where prepositions can be used is in directions, whether you are asking for directions – if you're a woman! – or giving them.

Asking and offering directions in Spanish

The thing about Spanish villages and towns is that there seem to be any number of roads in and out of the place. And not all businesses have a shiny new sign above the premises. And of course, if you're on holiday, it's all new to you anyway. So there's bound to come a time when you need to ask directions. Alternatively, someone may stop you in the street to ask directions of you, if you look as if you belong there. Here's how to deal with it.

One word you really need for directions is 'donde?' (where?) That's the magic key to unlock your directions, whether you're a couple of streets away from your destination, or several kilometres. Donde is always paired with está, since although you're asking about the fixed whereabouts of a theatre, museum, railway station or whatever, you're talking geographical locations, so the verb you want is Estar, rather than Ser. So you might well say '¿Donde está el museo?' (Where is the museum?)

Directions will involve going straight on (siga recto or todo recto), turning right or left (Gire a la derecha/ a la izquierda), and negotiating roundabouts. 'Turn right at the second roundabout' would be 'Gire a la derecha en la segunda rotunda.' Native speakers may dispense with the 'gire.'

If the directions involve using a main highway (autovia) it's handy to know the word for exit, which is salida.' Spanish highway exits don't follow a regular pattern of numbering, so just because you just passed Salida 730, you can't assume the next Salida will be 731. For this reason, exits are usually described by town, village or suburb. It's also worth remembering that just about every highway has directions for the capital, Madrid, so don't automatically assume you have gone wrong when you see Madrid marked up on the next Salida and you're travelling in the opposite direction!

Other useful direction words are norte (north), sur (south), este (east), and oeste (west). People won't necessarily use them when giving you directions, but if you're driving into a large town or city, you'll find there are several exits, and knowing the compass points will help you find the most appropriate one.

With just these few words, combined with prepositions and augmented by your vocabulary, you should be able to ask – and give – directions, and, more importantly, understand what is said to you.

Chapter 6
Using Reflexive Verbs

One of several ways in which the Spanish language differs from English is in the use of reflexive verbs. A reflexive verb is one which describes an action you do to yourself, for example, washing yourself. However, English speakers tend to say 'I have a bath,' or 'I take a shower.'

If you drop 'Tengo un baño' (I'm having a bath) into a Spanish conversation, it's likely you'll get a surprised look and a shrug of the shoulders, as much as to say, 'And your point is? ...' That's because to a native Spanish speaker, the phraseology means you possess a bath – along with everyone else. They would think you were a bit strange for drawing attention to the fact. And if you say 'I take a shower,' they might think you had turned to criminal activity, and were robbing your neighbor's bathroom while he was out!

If the mere mention of reflexive verbs gives you a headache, don't worry – once you have a grasp of regular verbs, you're already half way to using reflexive verbs. In fact, you've probably been using at least one reflexive verb without even realizing it. If you ask someone's name in Spanish, or if someone asks your name, it's '¿ Como se llama?' – literally, 'What do you call yourself?' This uses the formal form of the verb llamar (to call), since obviously you can't be familiar with someone whose name you don't even know. You would use the same form when asking the name of another person or pet, since the third person singular form of the verb is the same as the second person formal.

Conjugating reflexive verbs

The infinitive of a reflexive verb is the normal infinitive, plus the suffix 'se,' so to wash oneself would be 'lavarse.' To conjugate the verb, just drop the ending, conjugate as normal, and pair it with the appropriate reflexive pronoun. These are object pronouns rather than subject pronouns, because as well as doing the action – in this case washing – you are doing it to yourself. In other words, you are both the subject and the object of the verb.

Therefore if you want to tell someone you're performing your ablutions, you'd say 'Yo me lavo,' (I'm having a wash, or literally, I am washing myself). You can dispense with the subject (yo) and simply say 'Me lavo' and you will be understood. However, if you are washing your dog, there is no need for a reflexive verb or an object pronoun, since you (the subject) are performing the action on the dog (the object). So in this instance, you would simply say 'Lavo mi perro.' (I am washing my dog).

The table below is a sample conjugation of the reflexive verb lavarse, together with the appropriate object pronouns, which always go immediately before the verb. Literally, 'Yo me lavo' is 'I myself wash' in word order. The reflexive pronoun goes before the verb, in a similar way that adjectives go before nouns in Spanish, and you say 'Un vestido rojo' (A dress red) rather than 'A red dress.'

Spanish	English
Yo me lavo	*I wash myself*
Tú te lavas	*You wash yourself (informal)*
El/ella se lava	*He/she washes himself/herself*
Usted se lava	*You wash yourself (formal)*
Nosotros/as nos lavamos	*We wash ourselves*
Vosotros/as os laváis	*You wash yourselves*

	(plural informal)
Ustedes se lavan	*You wash yourselves (plural formal)*
Ellos/ellas se lavan	*They wash themselves*

As you can see, it's pretty straightforward to conjugate a reflexive verb, since it's the same conjugation as a present tense verb, with the addition of one of five reflexive pronouns – me, te, se, nos, os. There really is nothing to worry about!

Reflexive verbs are a feature of the Romance languages, and you really need to get a handle on them if you want to speak Spanish like the natives, but don't stress out about them. Anything you do for yourself – and talk about – is reflexive action. Getting up, going to bed, getting dressed, showering, bathing, cleaning your teeth and shaving all take the reflexive. The verb 'levantar,' which means 'to lift up,' changes meaning to 'to get up' in the reflexive form 'levantarse.' Here's how to use it:

Me levanto a las siete cada dia

I get up at 7 every day

As with all matters concerned with the Spanish language, if you practice using reflexive verbs, you will soon get the hang of them. The great thing about Spanish is that there are not too many pitfalls for the unwary. If you've worked your way through the chapters in this book, and practiced everything, you should now be confident enough to hold a basic conversation in Spanish.

Now you should aim to increase your vocabulary and delve deeper into verb tenses and pronoun use in order to improve your language skills and grow in confidence. Try to speak some Spanish every day, but above all, enjoy using this beautiful, expressive language.

Chapter 7
Spanish Language Quirks

Like any language, Spanish has its quirks and foibles, but it's very straightforward in a lot of ways, so these quirks shouldn't present you with too many problems. And there certainly are not so many as you find in the English language. It's not essential to learn about them, but just being aware of them will help you to become more proficient in the language, and help you to sound more like a local.

Apocopation

Apocopation is the practice of shortening some adjectives whenever they precede masculine nouns. Other than a few exceptions, apocopation never happens with feminine nouns, so as a quirky way to remind yourself when to apocopate, just say to yourself 'Cut a bit off the male.'

You may even have been apocopating without even realizing what you were doing. For example, if you go out for a snack at lunchtime, you may well ask for 'un bocadillo.' On the other hand, if you want to eat more healthily, you may order 'una ensalada.' The masculine 'uno' (meaning one) is the most common example of apocopation, and if you speak a little Spanish each day, you're almost certain to have used it in its shortened form.

'Bueno' – which means 'good' - is another common adjective that is always shortened with masculine nouns. So, when the waiter brings your lunch, he'll say 'buen provecho.' However, the guy in the Tabac who sells you your Euromillions lottery ticket will say 'buena suerte,' because suerte - meaning luck - is feminine, so there are no bits to cut off.

These are the most common short form adjectives:

- bueno - buen (good)

- malo - mal (bad)

- postrero - postrer (final, last)

- uno - un (one, a)

- primero - primer (first)

- tercero - tercer (third)

- alguno - algún (some)

- ninguno - ningún (none)

Other short form adjectives you need to know are grande, which becomes 'gran' when preceding both masculine and feminine nouns. Ciento (100) becomes 'cien' in certain instances, and cualquiera - meaning 'any' or 'whatever' - loses the 'a' at the end.

This is Spanish we're learning, so there is always something that goes against the rules and is different. Where apocopation is concerned, it's the word 'santo,' which means 'saint.' This is only shortened when it precedes certain proper nouns, but not those beginning with 'Do' or 'To.' So to be correct, you'd say 'San Juan,' and 'Santo Tomas.'

As a matter of fact, as you get used to the flow of the Spanish language, you'll find yourself automatically apocopating, simply because it sounds better as you speak. If you don't apocopate, nobody will die, so don't worry too much. However, if you do, you'll sound more like the native speakers, and ultimately, that's what you're aiming for.

Comparatives and superlatives

Making comparisons in Spanish is very different to the English way. In English, you'd simply say 'big, bigger, biggest,' where big is the standard adjective, bigger is a comparative, and biggest is the superlative. However, it doesn't work that way in Spanish.

Taking grande (big) as an example to compare like for like, there is no equivalent in Spanish of the –er and –est comparative and superlative. Instead, the language makes use of the words más (more) and menos (less). So, bigger is más grande (literally more big), and biggest is el más grande. (The more big, literally, which sounds rather odd to English or American ears, but makes perfect sense to Spanish speakers).

While you're not likely to use superlatives all that often, you could find yourself using comparatives more frequently than you might expect. For example, when shopping for clothing and shoes, you might need to ask for a smaller or larger size in something. Here are a couple of examples to illustrate comparatives in action.

¿Tienes esta falda en una taille más pequeña?

Do you have this skirt in a smaller size?

Quiero una taille más grande, por favour.

I would like a larger size, please.

Notice the word order – the noun (size) precedes the adjective (smaller/larger).

Older and younger

Another example of the use of comparatives is when saying one person is older or younger than another. The Spanish words for young and old are joven and viejo/vieja respectively. You may think 'más joven' is younger, and 'más viejo' is older, based on what you've just learned about Spanish comparatives, and while that is understandable, it's also wrong!

There are special comparative expressions for 'younger' and 'older', and they are 'menor que' and 'mayor que,' meaning 'younger than' and 'older than' respectively. Here are a couple of examples.

Maria es menor que su hermano

Maria is younger than her brother

Juan es mayor que Pedro

Juan is older than Pedro

Take some time to construct a few sentences using 'menor que' and 'mejor que,' using members of your family and friends – it's great practice, and it will help you to familiarize yourself with these comparatives.

Best and worst

The Spanish words for best and worst are 'mejor' and 'peor.' There's nothing quirky about that, but there is a slight difference in the way they work in speech and writing. As you surely know by now, in Spanish, the adjective follows the noun. This is not the case with major and peor. For example, if you are describing a shirt by color, you would say 'Mi camisa roja.' (My red shirt). However, if you were talking about your best shirt, you would say, 'Mi mejor camisa.' Here's how mejor and peor work in sentences.

Maria es la mejor estudiante en la classe

Maria is the best student in the class

Es la peor excusa de todas

That is the worst excuse of all

Las mejores cosas en la vida son gratis

The best things in life are free

él es el peor doctor en el hospital

He is the worst doctor in the hospital

Mejor and peor can also be preceded by 'lo' to mean 'the best/worst thing,' without the need to use the noun 'cosa.'

Double negatives

If you ever used a double negative in school, chances are your teacher was horrified. Not sure what a double negative is? Well, the Rolling Stones hit *I Can't Get No Satisfaction* is a good example. In English, double negatives are frowned upon because they cancel each other out. Mick Jagger should really sing 'I can't get any satisfaction,' to be grammatically correct. However, it's not quite so catchy, is it?

In Spain, the attitude to double negatives is much more relaxed. Rather than being viewed as a grammar sin, double negatives are believed to emphasize what you're saying. In fact, you may even come across a triple negative occasionally, because the Spanish do love to emphasize stuff!

In Spanish, if you want to say you are not doing something, you simply put 'no' in front of the conjugation – no means the same in both Spanish and English. Therefore, 'Tengo' is 'I have,' and 'No tengo' means 'I don't have.' Obviously, you need to identify what you do or do not have, and in the unfortunate case that you didn't have anything at all, you'd say 'No tengo nada.' (Literally translated, that's 'I don't have nothing, so it's a double negative. However, Spanish speakers would translate it as 'I don't have anything').

These are the 'negative' words you're most likely to come across:

Spanish	English
nada	*nothing*
nadie	*nobody*
ninguno/a	*none*
Nunca jamás	*never*
tampoco	*neither*
Ni ... ni	*Neither ... nor*

Use these words to come up with your own examples of double negatives. Here are a few to start you off.

No hay nada en el bolso

There is nothing in the bag

No necesito nada del mercadillo

I don't need anything from the market

No tengo ningunos libros

I don't have any books

You'll soon get used to using negatives in Spanish, because it comes naturally to use no with a negative word. Just remember not to make the translation literally, because that would cause confusion. Spanish negative words can have more than one meaning – particularly nada, which can be taken to mean 'nothing,' 'nothing at all,' or even 'anything' in certain contexts. It's worth going a little more deeply into Spanish negatives, so that you can talk like the locals do.

These are the most common Spanish language quirks you are likely to come across. There are others of course, but the intention of this book is to get you speaking Spanish quickly, so we're not going to bog you down with stuff you're hardly ever likely to use. Spend some time familiarizing yourself with the way these quirks work. In fact that's good advice at every stage of learning Spanish – get familiar with each new language skill before moving on to the next, and remember to revise as you go. Along with speaking or writing some Spanish every day, it's the best way to get it all fixed in your brain. Buena suerte!

Chapter 8
Numbers and Colors

Learning Spanish numbers and colors is a great way to increase your store of Spanish words and expand your conversational opportunities. Colors and numbers are things you can look up quickly and with ease, and there are no complicated grammar rules so some Spanish language books tend to leave them out. Also, numbers and colors are seen as something kids need to know, so some authors think including a section on the topic dumbs down the book. As a result, they are the 'poor relations' of the language, but this author happens to think numbers and colors should be included in any Spanish learning materials.

A sound knowledge of numbers and colors will help you to construct more complex sentences, ask and answer questions, and chip in with advice and comments in conversation. It detracts from your street cred if you need to look up the Spanish for number 8 – which is ocho – before you can finish your sentence, so spend a little time familiarizing yourself with Spanish numbers and colors. It's a nice little interlude among the irregular and reflexive verbs, personal 'a' and pronouns anyway!

Learning numbers and colors is also a good way to get children interested in learning Spanish, because there are lots of fun ways to fix the numbers and colors in their minds, and learning should always be fun. If you have a child or a grandchild, why not involve them in learning the simpler elements of Spanish with you? It will be fun for both of you, and it's great practice for you.

Numbers in Spanish

Spanish numbers are a pleasure to learn, because they are so simple to construct, once you have learned the basic numbers from 1 to 30, and the words for 40, 50, 60, 70, 80, 90 and the special terms for the hundreds. The only problem is if you should ever want to write out the words in full, because that can get a bit lengthy. Some of the high numbers can be a bit of a mouthful in Spanish too, so native speakers tend to shorten the process whenever they can. For example, instead of saying 'doscientos noventa y cuatro' for the number 294, a local would say 'dos-nueve-cuatro,' using the Spanish words for 2, 9 and 4.

Here are some tables to help you learn Spanish numbers. To help you with pronunciation, you can pull up an online number sheet from one of the reputable language learning sites. Click on the number, and there will be an audio with the correct pronunciation.

Numbers from 1 – 30

1 - uno	11 - once	21 - veintiuno
2 - dos	12 - doce	22 – veintidos
3 – tres	13 - trece	23 - veintitrés
4 - cuatro	14 - catorce	24 - veinticuatro
5 - cinco	15 - quince	25 - veinticinco
6 - seis	16 - dieciséis	26 - veintiséis
7 - siete	17 - diecisiete	27 - veintisiete
8 - ocho	18 - dieciocho	28 - veintiocho
9 - nueve	19 - diecinueve	29 - veintinueve
10 - diez	20 - veinte	30 - treinta

Just a couple of points of interest here. Notice that once you move into the teens and twenties, instead diez y seis and so on, there is the combined word dieciséis . That's because of grammar rules when certain letters follow each other in combination words. No need to stress over the details – just take it as fact! The other thing to notice is that tres and seis pick up a tilde (accent) in the combination numbers, which shortens the length of the vowels. You'll notice the difference if you listen to the numbers being pronounced in an audio clip. Again, it's nothing to be bothered about – it's just the way it is!

Numbers from 30 – 90

Each of the 'tens' numbers from 20 to 90 has a special name, and the single numbers from 11 to 30 are single word combinations of the diez or veinte + the relevant single number. Once you get past 30 though, the format changes to a regular pattern for every other Spanish number you construct. So, 31 is treinta y uno, 45 is cuarenta y cinco, 59 is cincuenta y nueve and so on, as high as you want to go. Once you have the special names for 40, 50, 60, 70, 80 and 90, you can count right the way up to 99 in Spanish.

40	cuarenta
50	cinquenta

60	sesenta
70	setenta
80	ochenta
90	noventa

Before you get into the hundreds, take some time to practice these numbers. A great way to practice is to get together with a few friends for a game of bingo. It doesn't matter if they don't know any Spanish, because you can be the caller, and you can first call the number in Spanish, then in English. Make learning numbers fun, and they will fall into place so much more quickly and easily.

Numbers from 100 – 1000

From 100 to 1000, each 'hundred' number has a special name. There's a bit of a quirk with 100, which is 'cien.' When you get to 101, it's 'ciento uno,' etc., until you get to 131, which is 'ciento treinta y uno.' The same pattern applies to 200s, 300s, and all the rest, just as in the low numbers. From 1 – 30, it's a single word, but from then on, 'y' comes into play.

Why do we go from cien to ciento? Who knows, but it certainly rolls off the tongue easier. 200 is doscientos, 201 is doscientos uno, and 231 is doscientos treinta y uno. Check out the 'hundred' numbers, and look out for 500 – it's different to the rest.

100	cien
200	doscientos
300	trescientos
400	cuatroscientos
500	quinientos
600	seiscientos
700	setecientos
800	ochocientos
900	novecientos
1000	mil

It gets a little more involved when you get into the high numbers, and in practice, you'd probably shorten them in speech. If you're booked into hotel room 575, you probably wouldn't say 'quinientos setenta y cinco,' you'd say 'cinco-siete-cinco.' However, it's good practice to work out numbers, whether randomly or in sequence.

Once you get past 1000 (mil), it still works in the same way. 1120 is 'mil ciento veinte.' 1132 is 'mil ciento treinta y dos. So now you can count up to 1999, if you're so inclined. 2000 is 'dos mil,' so if you want to say the current year in Spanish, it's 'dos mil dieciséis.' (2016). Spend some time playing around with numbers until it comes naturally to you – and it will, very soon.

Once you have a good grasp of numbers, you're good to go with all sorts of conversations. You can talk about the time, ask for specific quantities in shops and on the market, and even trot out continental shoe sizes. Mine is trienta y ocho (38, or UK size 5).

Colors

Knowing the names of colors is an essential element of learning any language. Color names are adjectives, and as such, they take on the gender of the noun they are describing, and are placed after that noun. So, a yellow dress would be 'Un vestido amarillo,' but a yellow skirt would be 'Una falda amarilla.' However, there are some exceptions - usually when the color name ends in a consonant – where the name is the same in masculine and femine genders. Some colors such as 'rosa' (pink) also only have one form for both genders.

Colors also take on plurals when they apply to more than one item. In the example above, '4 yellow dresses' would be 'cuatro vestidos amarillos.' When the color name ends in a consonant, the plural form adds 'es.' So you would say 'una camisa azul,' (a blue shirt), but 'Dos camisas azules' (two blue shirts). These irregularities need to be learned, as they are not always immediately apparent. However, don't stress about it. The world won't come to an end if you mess up on color plurals!

Colors are going to crop up repeatedly in conversation, and you'll struggle if you don't know them. Here's a list of some of the most common color names – read, learn and digest!

Spanish	English	Spanish	English
Rojo/a	red	azul	blue
Amarillo/a	yellow	Azul marino	Navy blue
rosa	pink	Azul cielo	Sky blue
verde	green	Plateado/a	silver
Negro/a	black	Dorado/a	gold
Blanco/a	white	Anaranjado/a	orange
gris	grey	morado	purple
marron	brown	lila	lilac

cafe	Dark brown	crema	cream

Two other words which might come in handy when discussing or describing colors are 'claro' –meaning 'light' and 'oscuro,' which means 'dark.' You now have a handy knowledge store of numbers and colors which will help you to understand more Spanish and also converse more.

This chapter covers the use of colors and numbers in Spanish. Many books don't bother with this, as they see it as rather simplified, but sometimes the simple things can make all the difference. Knowing your numbers and colors in Spanish will certainly make a difference to your understanding and use of the language.

Chapter 9

Getting Physical!

Learning Spanish is fun, and using it is even more fun, but sometimes, life gets serious, and you may need to visit a doctor or the hospital. You can save yourself a lot of worry – and the cost of hiring a translator – if you have a good working knowledge of parts of the body and medical terms. It's also a good idea to know about the different people who may be dealing with you when you're ill.

Knowing this sort of thing is what separates the casual, vacation Spanish speaker from those who are serious about learning the language. Okay, you may never need to use this knowledge – let's hope you don't – but it will give you a more thorough grounding in the language. And knowing something about your anatomy in Spanish could come in handy if you need to visit the Farmacia (drug store).

Body parts

Learning the Spanish names for the various parts of the body is useful in all kinds of situations. It helps you to explain to the doctor or pharmacist where your problem is, and that helps to get an accurate diagnosis and speedy treatment. In Spain, pharmacists are qualified to offer advice and prescribe medication for minor ailments. While many Farmacias have at least one English speaking person, if you find yourself in a tiny village miles from anywhere with a medical problem, you need to be able to communicate before the problem becomes an emergency.

Here, then, is a rundown of the body parts you'll need to know. To make it easier to learn, we've divided it into three sections – the head, the torso, and the limbs.

The head

Many health problems start in the head – and by that we don't mean imaginary illnesses! Headaches, hair loss, rashes on the face, toothache, earache, nosebleeds – okay, it's nothing life threatening, but these minor ailments can be very distressing. Here's the vocabulary you need for the parts of your head that may cause you problems.

Spanish	English
La cabeza	head

El cabello/ el pelo*	hair
La cara	face
La frente	forehead
La mejilla	cheek
La oreja/Las orejas	Ear(s)
El ojo/los ojos	Eye(s)
La nariz	nose
La boca	mouth
El labio/los labios	Lip(s)
El diente/os dientes	Tooth/teeth
La lengua	tongue
El cuello	neck
La garganta	throat

*Although el pelo is commonly used to mean 'hair,' strictly speaking it refers to body hair or animal fur, so el cabello is the correct word, although for many Spanish people, the two are interchangeable.

The torso

There are many Spanish terms for body parts in the torso, but it can all get very confusing, so we've kept it fairly simple here, and just included the most useful words in the list. Feel free to look up as many more as you want to!

Spanish	English
El tronco	torso
El pecho	chest
El abdomen/el estomago	stomach
La espalda	Back
El riñon/los riñones	Kidney(s)
La cadera/las caderas	hips
La cintura	waist
El higado	liver
El pulmon/los pulmónes	Lung(s)

The limbs

If you have any sort of joint problems, and you need to visit a doctor or the hospital, you're going to need to know the names of the various parts of the arms and legs. Here's a simple, straightforward guide to get you started.

Spanish	English
El brazo/los brazos	Arm(s)
La mano/los manos	Hand(s)
El dedo de la mano	Finger
El pulgar	thumb
La muñeca	wrist
El codo	elbow
La pierna	leg
La pantorilla	calf
La rodilla	knee
El muslo	thigh

El pie	foot
El tobillo	ankle
El dedo del pie	toe

These are pretty much all the words you'll need to make yourself understood at the Pharmacia, doctor's office or hospital. There are of course many other body part names in Spanish, and if you feel so inclined, by all means learn them. However, the aim of this book is to get you speaking Spanish as soon as possible, so we're giving you the main tools you need to get going.

There's something else you need to go with your newfound knowledge of Spanish anatomical terms, and that's the correct way to tell the nurse (enfermera) or doctor (medico) what hurts and where. And there's a special reflexive verb just made for that job!

The verb doler

The irregular verb 'doler' has several meanings, which can be confusing at first for native English speakers learning Spanish. It can mean 'to cause pain,' but the meaning of interest here is when the verb refers to the body part that's giving you problems, because that's what the doctor wants to know.

In this context, the verb means 'it hurts me,' or whoever is in pain. The 'it' referred to in the phrase is the body part. So, 'Me duele la garganta' – literal meaning 'My throat hurts me' – is what you'd say if you were unfortunate enough to be suffering from a sore throat. When explaining to the doctor that a family member or friend has a sore throat – perhaps because they can't speak Spanish, or they've lost their voice – it's 'se duele la garganta.' (He/she has a sore throat). If you're trying to find out what's wrong with a child, you'd ask '¿Te duele la garganta?' (Does your throat hurt? Or Is your throat sore?)

Notice that in all these examples, the body part does not take on a possessive. You don't say 'Me duele mi garganta,' because you've specified who is hurting with the pronoun in the first part of the sentence. It's clear that it's your throat that is sore, just as in the second example it's evident from the context that he (or she) has a sore throat. Sticking in a 'mi' or a 'su' is just overkill.

Another point to note is that if you're talking about your eyes, hands, ears, feet, legs – or anything you have more than one of which happen to be hurting - the verb becomes plural, although you still retain the first person pronoun. So, 'Me duelen las rodillas' means 'My knees are hurting.'

If you want to rule out a source of pain, just stick a 'no' at the start of the sentence. For example, 'No me duele el estomago' means 'My stomach doesn't hurt.'

Should you want to emphasize how badly your throat, knees or whatever are hurting, it's slightly different. Maybe you're in a lot of pain, so you'd say 'Me duelo mucho.' Notice the difference here? You're using first person reflexive, because you are experiencing a lot of pain, and you want to make that clear to the doctor, once you've identified the culprit.

Another useful pronoun to use with the verb doler is 'le,' which is a neutral pronoun meaning 'it.' That's handy if your questioning a child to find the source of the pain, and it will help to understand what the doctor is saying too.

If you're beginning to think all this is somewhat confusing, it isn't really, once you get to grips with the verb form and word order. Here are a few sentences, with translations, to get you into 'me duele' mode. If you're still feeling confused, why not try to construct a few sentences of your own? It's great practice, and you never know when you might need them.

Spanish	English
Me duele la pierna	*My leg hurts*
Me duelen las piernas	*My legs hurt*
¿Donde te duele?	*Where do you hurt/ are you hurting?*

¿Donde le duele?	*Where does it hurt?*
Me duele el pecho cuando respiro profundo	*My chest hurts when I breathe deeply*
Me duele mucho el pecho	*My chest hurts a lot*
Se duelen las rodillas y los pies	*His knees and his feet hurt*
Me duele cuando corro	*It hurts when I run*

In summary, the pronouns you will need most often with the verb doler are 'me, se, le and te.' The verb is always third person 'duele,' unless you are referring to something you have more than one of, such as eyes and hands, when it becomes 'duelen.' Note that if you are talking of pain in two locations where one is singular and the other is plural, you would say 'Me duele la cabeza y me duelen las piernas tambien.' (I have a headache and my legs hurt as well). That should be enough to tell the doctor that you're probably coming down with flu!

It's worth spending some time with doler and familiarizing yourself with the various ways of explaining your ailments – or someone else's. As in all things Spanish, the more you practice, the more familiar it becomes, so if you prepare yourself ahead of the necessity, you should be able to deal with the situation calmly.

Using tener – alone or with dolor

If you're confident with the names of body parts in Spanish, but you're still a bit wary of using 'doler' to explain your ailments, you can ease yourself into it gradually by using the verb tener (to have) with the nound 'dolor' (pain, ache). As you may remember from earlier in the book, tener is a regular verb which is often used in personal contexts. You will say 'tengo hambre' (literally 'I have hunger') when you are hungry, and if someone asks your age, you'll reply 'tengo 30 años,' or whatever. Here's a reminder of how tener conjugates.

Tener

Yo tengo

Tú tienes

Él/ella/usted tiene

Nosotros venemos

Vosotros tenéis

Ellos/ellas/ustedes tienen

When using 'tener' in health-related expressions, you would say, for example, 'Tengo dolor de la cabeza.' (I have a headache). So basically, any of the expressions you've learned using 'me duele' can also be used with 'tener + dolor + de.' There is no right or wrong here – it's whatever you are most comfortable with.

Knowing the verb tener is also handy for describing certain ailments more clearly. For example, if you have a broken leg, clearly it is very painful, but if you actually heard the bone crack, you can speed up the diagnosis by saying 'Tengo la pierna rota' rather than just 'Me duele la pierna.' If you're not certain the bone is broken, tack on 'Pienso que.' (I think that ...)

Here are a few examples where tener can be used most effectively to describe symptoms and conditions. English translations are included for simplicity.

Spanish	English
Tengo resfriado	I have a cold
Tengo gripe	I have flu
Tiene la fiebre/la calentura	He/ she has a fever
¿Tienes la fiebre?	Do you have a fever?
Tengo tos	I have a cough

Pienso que tiene el brazo roto	I think he has a broken arm.

Once you have learned most of these expressions, you should be able to communicate your medical problems in a way that will help the health professionals dealing with your case to arrive at a speedy diagnosis. In fact, it may be worth making a list of the most common ailments, and also any particular medical problems you may have yourself. It all makes it so much calmer and easier when the need for treatment arises.

At the hospital

Worst case scenario, you end up at Urgencias (Emergency Room, Casualty Department. So, where does it go from here? Hopefully, you're up to date on your body parts and all the 'it hurts' stuff. Anyway, here's what to expect from a visit to the hospital in Spain.

There are three bits of good news here – there's plenty of free parking in Spanish hospitals, and hospital is the same in both English and Spanish. Most importantly of all, the standard of care and cleanliness in the Spanish health care system is exemplary.

Spain is big on bureaucracy, and it's no different at the hospital. There will be paper work to complete before you get to the waiting room, where just one person will be able to accompany you. Unless you speak Spanish yourself, the person accompanying you should be a Spanish speaker, if possible. Once you've shown ID and given the required information, you'll be assessed by an enfermera (nurse), who will decide on the urgency of your case.

If you have an unspecified or undiagnosed pain or problem, you might tell the nurse 'No me siento bien.' (I'm feeling unwell), or 'Me siento mal' (I feel ill). You may even say 'Me siento débil,' (I feel weak). Or of course, you can use one of the 'me duele' or 'tengo dolor' phrases.

Once you get to see the doctor, he'll want to know your symptoms. We've already covered how to explain various pains, but here are some useful phrases to help you to communicate your symptoms in Spanish.

Spanish	English
Pienso que es una ataque cardiaco	*I think it's a heart attack*
Sangro mucho	*I'm bleeding a lot*
Vomito cada vez como	*I vomit every time I eat*
Estoy siempre cansado	*I am always tired*

Tengo la insolación	*I have sunstroke*
Tengo una alergia	*I have an allergy*
Mi tipo de sangre es ...	*My blood type is...*

There are also some phrases el medico (the doctor) may use to you, so here's a brief run down of the most common things you'll hear.

Spanish	English
¿Que sintomas tiene?	*What symptoms do you have?*
¿Ha tenido estos sintomas antes?	*Have you had these symptoms before?*
¿Ha tenido este dolor antes?	*Have you had this pain before?*
¿Tome alguna medicina?	*Are you taking any medication?*
¿Puede orinar?	*Are you able to urinate?*
¿Está entreñido?	*Have you been*

	constipated?
¿Puedo chequear su pulso?	*May I check your pulse?*
¿Puedo chequear su presión?	*May I check your blood pressure?*
¿Puedo tomar su temperatura?	*May I take your temperature?*
Respire profundo	*Breathe in deeply*
Tose, por favor	*Cough, please*
Abre su boca, por favor	*Open your mouth, please*

These symptoms, combined with the earlier phrases, should get you through most situations. If you have a particular health condition which may necessitate regular hospital visits, it is well worth looking up the specific vocabulary to help you get through a visit to a Spanish hospital.

If you have a potentially serious health condition, it's worth asking your own doctor for a letter in Spanish to carry with you, explaining any problems that may arise. Most health centers will provide a translation for a modest cost, or even free of charge.

The doctor's questions should not present a problem either. If you find he is speaking too quickly, say, 'Habla más despacio, por favour.' (Speak more slowly, please). While nobody relishes a trip to the hospital, you'll find the staff at Spanish hospitals – like all Spanish people – are friendly and helpful.

At the Farmacia

As has been mentioned earlier, pharmacists in Spain are qualified to offer advice and recommend treatment for minor ailments. You can even get some prescription medications over the counter in Spain, including antibiotics. The main word you need for the farmacia is 'Necesito' – 'I need.' That will get you a long way, and here are some of the things you may need from the farmacia.

Spanish	English
Necesito jarabe por tos	*I need cough syrup*
Pienso que he comido algo que en mal estado	*I think I've eaten something bad*
Tengo diarrea	*I have diarrhoea*
Necesito esta medicina	*I need this medicine*
¿Tienes algo para ...?	*Do you have something*

	for...?
Necesito la tiritas	*I need plasters*
Necesito medicamento para el dolor/ el resfriado/ el dolor de estomago	*I need painkillers/ cold medicine/ stomach medicine*
Tengo presion alta/baja	*I have high/low blood pressure*
Tengo problemas a respirar	*I am having difficulty breathing*

These phrases should help you out at the farmacia, whatever your problems. However, there is one thing you should be aware of. The farmacia in Spain is a social meeting point as much as a health service, so don't expect any sense of urgency at all, unless you collapse on the floor! Farmacias are happy, friendly places, and you will me made welcome and helped with your health problems, but you could be in for a long wait!

Let's face it, vocabulary for sickness is like health insurance – everyone hopes they won't need to use it! However, since accidents and illnesses are a fact of life – even when on vacation – it's a necessary component of your Spanish knowledge store. Familiarize yourself with the names of various body parts, and the more common questions and statements you are likely to come across at the farmacia, the doctor's office or the hospital. As an added precaution, take along a bilingual Spanish/English dictionary. You know it makes perfect sense!

Chapter 10
Spanish Food and Drink

The Spanish are rightly proud of their culinary heritage, and since their style of cuisine is the inspiration behind the Mediterranean Diet, it's also one of the healthiest ways of eating in the world. Spanish cuisine relies on cooking healthy, seasonal ingredients from scratch, with little or no processed foods finding their way into the typical Spanish diet. They are also big advocates of taking time over eating, so not only are you unlikely to suffer indigestion after a typical Spanish meal, you'll probably eat less, since it takes the brain around 20 minutes to send out 'full up' signals from the appetite center. The Spanish style of eating is therefore compatible with healthy eating and necessary weight loss. It's delicious too!

In this chapter, we'll look at the vocabulary you need to eat out in Spanish restaurants, and follow the instructions in Spanish recipes. Then you can enjoy practicing your Spanish over a leisurely meal. Is there any better way to learn a new language? It's unlikely! And of course, eating in Spain also involves drinking, so we'll look at some of the more common drinks, and how they are served.

Meal times in Spain

One thing you'll notice about meal times in Spain is that dinner (cena) is served very late. Spanish people tend to have a small breakfast (desayuno), followed by a long, leisurely lunch (almuerzo or comida

) between 2.00 and 4.00 pm, which means they're not ready for cena until at least 9.00 pm – or more likely later. That's why they don't need more than a tostada or churros and chocolate for breakfast. Churros are similar to doughnuts, except they're cooked in long strips, and tostada is toasted bread served with olive oil, tomatoes or jam.

Eating out in Spain

When you're eating out in Spain, look out for the Menu del Dia, or menu of the day. It's a set meal of three or four courses with wine, and it offers great choice and even better value.

Spain is also famous for its tapas – small servings of hot and cold dishes which can be enjoyed with a drink, or you may want to order a selection of tapas for lunch. Here are the words you need to help you navigate the menu in a Spanish restaurant, whatever the time of day.

Spanish	English	Spanish	English
cerdo	pork	Vacuno/ternera	beef
cordero	lamb	pavo	turkey
pollo	chicken	pato	duck
conejo	rabbit	huevos	eggs
gambas	prawns	mariscos	seafood
mejillones	mussels	calamares	squid
atun	tuna	pulpo	octopus
lenguado	sole	trucha	trout
bacalao	cod	almejas	clams
cangrejo	crab	dorada	bream
lentejas	lentils	queso	cheese
Habas/alubias	beans	pan	bread
albondigas	meatballs	acietunas	olives

zanahorias	carrots	arroz	rice
guisantes	peas	ensalada	salad
cebollas	onions	salsa	sauce
estofado	stew	sopa	soup

Most meat and fish is likely to be served 'asado/al horno' – which is roasted or baked in the oven, 'a la plancha' – grilled, or 'frier' – fried. Fish andseafood in particular is often served 'al vapor' (steamed). Or your meat or fish could be served up in a delicious estofado (stew). And if any of the dishes are marked 'casero' – particularly desserts – go for it, because it means they are home-made, often by the madre (mother) of the house.

You'll find that starters and appetizers in Spanish restaurants – 'primer plato' – come in rather large servings, while the 'plato principal' (main course) is usually meat or fish with a few fries or potatoes, and no vegetables to speak of. However, it's normal to start the meal with a salad, and bread with ali oli (garlic mayonnaise), so you won't go short on vitamins and fiber. And there's often fresh fruit for 'postre' (dessert).

Here are a few helpful phrases for making a reservation and ordering your meal. Eating out is a great way to practice your Spanish, and the waiters will be pleased that you made the effort, so you'll get great service.

Spanish	English
Quiero reservar una mesa para seis personas a las ocho, por favor	*I'd like to reserve a table for 6 people at 8 o'clock, please*
La carta/ la lista de vinos, por favor	*The menu/ wine list please*
Estoy listo para ordinar ahora	*I'm ready to order now*
I prefer my steak rare/ medium/ well done	*Prefiero la carne poco cocida/ a medio cocer/ bien cocida*
¿Hay un plato vegetariano, por favor?	*Is there a vegetarian choice, please?*
Quiero más pan/ vino/ agua	*I'd like more bread/ wine/ water*
La cuenta, por favor	*The bill, please*

It's quite likely that your waiter will speak some English- particularly if you're eating in a large city or resort, but don't be shy – use the Spanish you've learned to make your dining out experiences more authentic. And don't expect to leave the restaurant in less than two hours – the Spanish like to savor their food, and they expect everyone else to do the same – that's why they serve bread, olives and ali oli followed by salad.

It's all part of the unique, leisurely dining experience, and the good news is, no matter how much you eat, you're not likely to suffer from indigestion, since the food is spread over such a long time. Relax, chat, and enjoy the food – there'll be no pressure to finish so someone else can have the table. Once you book a table in a Spanish restaurant, it's yours for the duration.

Following Spanish recipes at home

While dining out in Spain is a great experience, sometimes you just want to chill out at home and experiment with Spanish recipes yourself. And you don't need a lot of Spanish to do that, or to be a particularly proficient cook. Typical Spanish recipes rely on just a few quality ingredients, simply cooked to allow the flavors to come through loud and clear.

Spanish cooking terms

Here's some basic cooking vocabulary to get you started. Where timings are concerned, they will be given in 'minutos' – minutes – or 'horas' (hours). Measurements will be in milliliters or liters and grams, so if you are accustomed to using Imperial measurements – pints, quarts, ounces, etc. – you'll need a conversion table handy.

Spanish	English	Spanish	English
cuchara	tablespoon	cubrir	cover
cucharilla	teaspoon	calentar	heat up
Cortar en lonchas finas/ gruesas	Slice thinly/ thickly	lavar	wash
cazuela	Earthenware oven proof dish	sarten	Frying pan
Cortar en cuadritos	diced	combinar	combine
picar	chop	rebozar	Coat (with flour,breadcr umbs)
doblar	Fold (eggs,etc. Folded into mixture)	batir	whisk
tritutar	liquidize	hacer puré	mash

Dejar en adobo	marinate	mezclar	mix
pelar	peel	vertir	pour
pizca	Pinch (of spices)	aplanar	Roll out
sofreir	Sauté, fry lightly	sazonar	season
hervir	boil	Cocinar a fuego lento	simmer

Notice all those words ending in –ar, -er and –ir? That's verbs in infinitive form, soyou'll get some more practice with conjugation. Usually, recipes will use the formal second person (usted) form of the verb, but as long as you know the infinitive, you'll be able to work out the instructions.

This list includes most of the most common cooking terms and measurements, but it's a good idea to have a dictionary handy, in case there are any surprises in store. Since most Spanish recipes are simple, with just a few key ingredients, you don't need an extensive vocabulary to follow them.

Common recipe ingredients

Spanish cuisine is not particularly rich or spicy, although certain herbs feature significantly. Many of the basic words for various meats, fish, seafood and vegetables have already been covered in the Eating Out section, but here are some of the common ingredients in Spanish recipes. Many of them are store cupboard items, so it's worth making a 'lista de compras' (shopping list) to stock up on the essentials before your first foray into the world of Spanish cuisine.

It's worth a special mention here about tomatoes. For culinary purposes, there are three kinds – 'troceado,' which are chopped plum tomatoes in a can, 'entero' – whole canned plum tomatoes – and 'tomate frito.' This is a type of tomato puree which can be used in various ways, and it's at the heart of many Spanish recipes.

Spanish	English	Spanish	English
Ajo/ diente de ajo	Garlic/ garlic clove	garbanzos	Chick peas
canela	cinnamon	Harina de trigo/ harina de maiz	Flour/ cornflour
albahaca	basil	nata	cream

eneldo	dill	almendras	almonds
gengibre	ginger	Pan rallado	breadcrumbs
menta	mint	caldo	Broth, stock
Nuez moscada	nutmeg	mantequilla	butter
perejil	parsley	Aciete de oliva/girasol	Olive/ sunflower oil
pimentón	paprika	Clara de huevo	Egg white
sal	salt	Yema de huevo	Egg yolk
pimienta	pepper	puerro	leek
romero	rosemary	Rabo de buey	oxtail
azafrán	saffron	shallot	cebolleta
tomillo	thyme	agridulce	Sweet and sour
calabacin	Courgette,	boniato	Sweet potato

	zucchini		
solomio	Pork tenderloin	bocadillo	sandwich
espinacas	spinach	vinagre	Vinegar

These ingredients should enable you to cook a good selection of Spanish recipes. As always, it's a good idea to keep a dictionary handy for those unfamiliar words. To make the experience more authentic, why not read up on special Spanish cooking techniques? Learning the language is so much easier when you immerse yourself in the culture.

Drinking in Spain

While the Spanish love to drink, and bars serve alcohol all day, there is no binge drinking culture in Spain, and you're unlikely to see excessive behavior as a result of enthusiastic alcohol consumption. That's because Spanish people tend to take food with their drink, rather than just going out for a drink.

The Spanish verb for 'to drink' is 'beber,' and the noun for drink is 'bebida.' That applies to any drink, whether alcoholic or not. It's also common to use the verb 'tomar' (to take) in a bar situation. More often than not, there is table service, unless it's a small chiringuito or cantina manned by one person, so the waiter will ask one of these questions:

¿Qué quieres tomar?

¿Qué desea tomar?

¿ Qué quieres beber?

¿Algo para beber?

The first three, loosely translated, mean the same thing 'What would you like to drink?' while the last phrase is 'Something to drink?' Whichever expression is used, reply using the same verb, so it's either 'Quiero una cerveza' or 'Deseo una cerveza,' either of which means 'I'd like a beer.' Not a beer drinker? Then here's the vocabulary you need to order anything you fancy in a Spanish bar. It's a good chance to practice your numbers, too, if you're part of a group

Spanish	English	Spanish	English
Agua natural/ con gas	Still/ sparkling water	Vino blanco/ rosado/ tinto	White/rose/red wine
Zumo de naranja/ manzana/ piña	Orange/ apple/ pineapple juice	sidra	cider

Gaseosa	Unsweetened fizzy lemonade	Vino de Jerez	sherry
limonada	Cloudy lemonade	Cerveza sin alcohol	Alcohol free beer
cerveza	beer	ron	rum
ginebra	gin	clara	shandy

Whisky, vodka and brandy are the same in Spanish as in English. However, unless you specify a brand, you will be served with locally produced spirits, which may not be quite what you expect. Whisky and cognac drinkers may not be happy with the Spanish versions, although there are some excellent ones around. Spanish spirit measures are also much more generous than you may be used to, so be careful out there!

When ordering beer, you can specify whether you want 'una botella' – a bottle – or 'cerveza de barril'(draught beer). If you just want a small draught beer, ask for a 'caña,' which is the smallest size the bar serves. A 'tanque' is usually around a pint, or you can simply ask for 'una cerveza grande' – 'a large beer.' Be advised that beers in Spain are usually from 4.5 – 5.5% alcohol by volume (ABV), so they may be stronger than you are accustomed to. If you want the taste and refreshing cooling power of the beer, without the high alcohol content, ask for a clara – a shandy made with beer and lemonade.

Soft drinks are known as 'refrescos,' but it's usual to order them by their brand names. As well as the internationally known brands, you'll see a lot of Kas and Fanta in Spain. Low calorie soft drinks are usually called light, rather than diet, so you'd ask for Coca Cola Light, or Sprite Light.

Coffee in Spain

You'll notice coffee doesn't appear in the vocabulary list above. That's because there are a number of ways to serve it, so it merits a paragraph or two of its own. The Spanish are passionate about their coffee, so be clear what you want. The most popular coffee in bars is 'café con leche' or coffee with milk, and it – like most other coffees – is freshly made in the machine. 'café solo' is the Spanish equivalent of espresso, and if you want a dash of milk in it, it's 'café cortado.' If it's a hot day, you might like a 'café con hielo.' That's an espresso served with a glass of ice, and the idea is to pour the coffee over the ice before drinking. If you want a large black coffee, it's 'café Americano.'

If decaffeinated coffee is your preference, prepare to be regarded with disbelief, before being offered a sachet of instant decaf with hot water. However, some establishments will offer 'Café descafeinado en la maquina' – that's decaffeinated coffee from the machine, in an attempt to give the tourists what they want, because it's usually tourists who order decaf!

It's not unusual for coffee to be served with brandy in Spain – even at breakfast time, so don't be surprised to see a group of locals gathered around a table with coffees and large brandies. Why not join them? After all, when in Spain ...

By now, you should be familiar with the foods and drinks of Spain, as well as feeling confident about ordering in bars and restaurants. Experiment with the flavors available to you, and enjoy the legendary Spanish hospitality. You've worked hard all the way through this book, and hopefully learned enough Spanish to be able to converse with confidence, so it seems entirely appropriate to end on a more relaxing note. Salud! (Cheers!)

Conclusion

Learning Spanish doesn't have to be difficult. Although in some aspects it is very different to English – for example in the use of the Personal A and reflexive verbs – the rules of engagement are often much simpler. There are not so many homophones – words that sound the same but have different meanings and may have different spellings – to get confused over, and the grammar rules are not so stringent. Pronunciation and spelling is phonetic, so that part is easier too.

A basic grasp of Spanish will ensure you can make yourself understood in many countries in the world, so if you're considering learning another language, Spanish is probably the most useful one to go for. There may be variations in different countries – Latin American Spanish is considerably different, but a good grasp of Castilian Spanish should ensure you are understood in most Spanish speaking countries.

Once you are confident with reading and conversing in Spanish, you will discover that it is a very vibrant and expressive language which is great fun to use. Native Spanish speakers tend to use their whole bodies in conversation, not just their voices, and the experience can be quite exhilarating, if a little intimidating at first. It can get rather loud, so you may think a fight is about to break out in the bar, when in fact it's just the locals enjoying good conversation!

The essential key to learning Spanish quickly and improving your speaking and writing skills is to use it often – every day if possible. Practice your new found skill until it becomes almost second nature, and you find yourself actually thinking in Spanish rather than translating from English before you begin to speak. Above all, experiment and have fun with this beautiful, expressive Romance language. Buena suerte!

Finally, if you received value from this book, then I would like to ask you for a favor. Would you be kind enough to leave a review for this book on Amazon?

Thank you so much!

Made in the USA
San Bernardino, CA
03 February 2018